FIRE IN MY
BONES

FIRE IN MY BONES

OLLIE MARSHALL-RICO

Ollie Marshall-Rico
Website: OllieMaeMarshall.Com
olliemarshallrico@yahoo.com
OllieMarshall07@gmail.com
(973)675-3277

Printed in the United States of America.

Library of Congress Control Number: 2024904005

ISBN: 979-8-89021-316-7 Paperback

ISBN: 979-8-89021-317-4 Hardback

ISBN: 979-8-89021-315-0 eBook

CONTENTS

Introduction and Part I

Fire in My Bones views the soul inside out with a profound inner spirit of society. It takes you through personal experiences with a harsh observation glimpse of this society. When power forces have glutted this poet's sanity, there is only one way out, and she dances her madness through the words of poetry. Until another time, perhaps, bit of her sanity remains, thread thin, but release comes, if only just for a moment. She has found her forces of strength with tissue laced on thorns. She holds tightly, knowing her sanity depends on that giv- en moment. She faces the forces---society's demons— and she prances with a howling inner cry.

Shall this day be her extinction? With each move she takes; it appears to be the final one. She keeps moving daring not to quit. Retraces are not allowed in this race; to do so could mean the extinction of her existence. She inhales and exhales. Straining to survive, she breathes, as Part I of the text commences.

Help me breathe, sister, I need to breathe!
My senses are dangling on rope's edge.
Your endurance will sustain my survival!

Part I

Sister, Help Me Breathe
Boxed Loneness
Breathing
Rage
Step By Step
No More
The Edge
My Soul
Happiness
Escape
Hate
Bloodline
Farewell

Part I

Sister, Help Me Breathe

Boxed Loneness

There is a loneness within me, separated from others.

A naked bone crying for its lost meat.

It begs in silent.

Although, longing desperately to be connected, the bone remains bare.

It's a free bone, a world of its own.

Yes, it's free, lacking the ability to connect to the whole or even one.

It's a game of self, an infinite river game, never ending.

The deepness of the unique bond sought not.

A truly mind game of self.

A jump rope pattern, endlessly decades.

It continues to walk that bare wither stream.

A sadness that cries over and over without the tools to put it at rest.

Breathing

Help me breathe, sister, I need to breathe.

The days are long and the night are short.

The music is low and the voices are high on the row.

My senses are dangling on rope's edge.

Help me breathe, sister, I need to breathe.

Take my hand to sustain me; the sand is too grainy, the blissful sun merciless.

Quick sand has stiffened the body to a pill kill.

Trying has sunk to a dying cry.

Help me breathe, sister, I need to breathe. Take this day and make me tomorrow.

Let your energy become mines; forces cannot be meet without your strength,

Your endurance will sustain my survival.

Help me to breathe, sister, I need to breathe.

This frail body need not be broken.

With your body anchored on solid shore, you can take this mind and make it strong.

Your endurance will sustain my survival. Your endurance will create my new song. Help me breathe, sister, I need to breathe!

GRAN CARIBE
grupo hoteleru

Rage

Cage man you have taken my humanity.
My emotions are distorted into rage.
You murder me and escape without a paid price.
You pull me off the street, just to call me thief.

Cage man you have taken my humanity.
Tree justice has given way to you.
You high-tech lynch me and call it justice.
From the Indian trumping system, your goal is tightly intact.

Cage man you have taken my humanity.
Express or acknowledge it not, race underlies your actions.
The Simpson saga overshadowed the President's State of the Union Address.
Perhaps her world of drugs and sex carved her grave, but you pay, mingling roots speaks.

Cage man you have taken my humanity.
Where has this human in me escaped.
You cruel and brutal acts have created this monster in me.
A moment of peace surrounds me only in a child's dream.

Step by Step

I cried in pain, trying to understand.
Step by step, he led me.
Capturing the heart through those emotions.
No remorse thought, phase one joyfully rewarded.

I cried in pain, trying to understand.
The Holy Word combined us as one.
No remorse thought, phase two, paper acknowledged.
Time ticked on scheduled.

I cried in pain, trying to understand.
Family travel money issued.
Visas delayed; permanent status procedures processed without complications.
No remorse thought, phase three, processed as planned.

I cried in pain, trying to understand.
Physical abuses, tribal community ladies confessed great friendship.
The male having controlled each act thrown on the stage.
No remorse thought, phase four, permanent status issued.

I cried in pain, trying to understand.
Love stood at the door, yet it was time to bid farewell.

Fire In My Bones

No remorse thought, phase five, wife eliminated.
Confused, buffed, and shocked, answer not there.

I cried in pain, trying to understand.
Street language was I, empty words dangled in the storm.
Fist a sword to harm.
No remorse thought, phase six, Pandora's Box opens.

I cried in pain, trying to understand.
This intensity trapped self-imposed involvement relationship to acquire permanent status allowed me to realize joy had been mines.

Financial gains stood no more; a call to action was upon me.
Painful it was, love went deep, yet dehumanization could be no more.

-11-

No More

Cast this unwanted body no more.

There are no more irons, only frails of paper blowing through the wind.

The power to exist has been discarded as useless.

All wounds have been patched and repatched until there is no more room for incisions.

Cast this unwanted body no more.

The Edge

What do you do when your whole darn world crashes at once?

Your friends are nesting in a cocoon.

Lack of understand with your family has separated you with distance.
Mindless adults have programmed children into vandalizing symbols
that you hold dear.

The individual who shared your bed last night understands you as a
Klansman understands a socialist.

Lack of courage will not permit you to stop the blood in your veins
from running.

So, what do you when your whole world crushes at once?
You move one step at a time, hoping the storm blows soon.

The Soul

Yesterday, my heart was filled with discontentment, because I knew you had a soul wandering for freedom.

One that has seen many lands and one that will search many more, and still wander.

A soul that will feel aroused to plunder for a short time, but restless not to be enchanted.

A soul that has the depth of feeling.

One that controls the vital parts of my spirit but never desires to possess the power it holds over this body.

One that has given compassion, love, and understanding to each traveler on the road except his inner self.

A soul that wanders as the Nile River, free and unrestrained from mankind.

Yesterday, discontented wandering thoughts filled my mind as the absence of your presence continuously grew closer.

A soul shall search the whole world through to find in a hundred years the answer at its own doorstep.

Yet, it will wander still, filling other's ears with worldly knowledge.

Happiness

As a plant flourishes in the sun, your kindness, warmth, and understanding generates in man.

Gracefully, as the golden sun disappears slowly, leaving the joy of pleasure upon the earthly bodies, you will always have a prominent place with those you have touched.

As an incandescent heavenly body centering on a solar system, your path is filled with joy and happiness for mankind.

Man cannot reciprocate that happiness and love which flourish from your total being.

A gift more precious than gold, many have pursued this path only to create a treadmill.

The contented mind that you bring to others will one day be your happiness.

-15-

Escape

The door opened, and he appeared as a dragonfly—a small, slender body, tall as a giant.

The room begins to flourish with opened eyes, as static heads begin to move.

When he smiled, the room twinkled with a star, engrossing the encageable.

Hate

My mind possess the power to hate as it does to love.

When the world turns to me with pain and you are not there to console me, I begin to hate you.

The thought of your warm touch on a cold winter night becomes repulsive.

I loathe the thought of having fallen in love with you.

Bloodline

Years will come and go; words will be unspoken.
A cluster of clouds will hang treading on hate lines.
Sisterhood hounds pound not at the door.
Companionship exists not.
Bloodline sisters focusing miles apart, with no returnable thoughts.
Tragedy forbidden through bloodline.
The bell tolls, the florist profits not.

Farewell

It is time to say farewell, my love.

So, travel well with those you choose.

Let there be no tearful farewell.

This departure only expresses good wishes.

This is not to proclaim the time we spent together left many pleasant memories; but it was an important transition period within my life.

Not one of smoothness, but a profound stage of development.

One that formed and conditioned a state of being within me. So goodbye, my love, and travel well with those you choose.

Part II

Part II highlights bonding. It gropes the dynamic of human interaction. It shows how strong bonds can become tissue thin, yet glue layered. Anchored into one's heritage, one sometimes fights to become a human being.

One should remember to trudge softly and dance easily with whose path you share because tomorrow is never the same as today, and today cannot undo yesterday's stones.

"Forever weakness, there is strength unseen."

Part II

Bonding
The Family
Breaking Loose
Silent Code
Mind Set Friend
Two Steps
Friendship
Dance

The Family

Destruction through separation, but the bond did not break.
Brave warriors forbidden through the slave system.
Operation with separation, limited the mothering cry.
Prowling, why, meant to die.

Destruction through separation, but the bond did not break.
An empty meal to feed the weak, kin separated by the color of skin.
Cotton tons, prevented pond fishing.
Family intimacy denied; slave-master's lust prevailed.

Destruction through separation, but the bond did not break.
The freedom movement brought out Harriet.
Street gangs, crack heads, teenage mothers, slave minds must be awakened.
Curb community genocide, the family must not break.

Destruction through separation, but the bond did not break.
Sisters, brothers, hold hands, the family must continue.
Crossing the tracks rejects your inner beauty.
The chains links have weakened greatly, the rain must stop.

Breaking Loose

It pains leaving these memories, crying, dying on make-believe
memories.

Take a rest and let the sea breeze cool.

Let the piece bridge the whole while the valley move on.

Make-believe memories, happy, glowing, strutting, popping, icing—
never memories.

Silent Code

-25-

Ministers holding their breath while due process escapes.

Voice silent on suspension denies due pension.

Terminated jobs eliminated functional roles.

Devastated minds meditated for answers.

Ministers holding their breath while due process escapes.

Murder threatens homicides, unable to cope, today's suicide.

How can your voice remain silent?

Are their pains in vain?

Ministers holding their breath while due process escapes.

Without a spoken word, how can a shepherd watch the slaughter of his sheep?

Are your hands intertwined so tightly that you would allow your sheep to die alone?

Will you be that leader who is demanded on your shore?

Ministers holding their breath while due process escapes.

Does your silence speak strong condemnation of the accused?

Judge not your enemy, guide your sheep, a strong silent disapproval.

A shepherd needs his sheep, but will the sheep sustain and maintain life through the scriptures?

Mind Set

There must be an application of the mind to endearment, brothers. The soul must be restored, and the spirit renewed through rejuvenation.

Every generation must reinforce the life and strength of the people. Goals must be implemented to rebuild and receive the fertility of the family.

Leaders must refresh their minds to create positive energy within the community.

Social relations must be carried out harmoniously with the past, the present and the future.

Commitment on ethical values must be spiritually rooted.

Brotherhood and sisterhood must demonstrate love through total involvement.

Quality human relations must be viewed through truth, harmony, justice and peace.

The application of endearment must be constantly mobilizing.

Friend

Today you shunned me when I needed you most.

My feelings became a mashed potato.

How will you treat me tomorrow if I permit you in.

You felt pain not when you pranced my story to the world.

Today you shunned me when I needed you most.

Center stage you craved while I hid in the cave.

Blind weakness, you stood tall, put me on the will.

Nature cried; do not capture in that manner.

Today you shunned me when I needed you most.

As my heart cried repeatedly, your spear plunge deepened.

When my sunny blue clouds became midnight, you put me in your
funny box.

To befriend you would elevate my weakness.

Today you shunned me when I needed you most.

Yesterday's departure lingers, it must come.

Separation most difficult; self-stagnation cannot anchor anymore.

Friends we are not; sister blending, yes; respectfully we greet.

Dance

Come, come, dance with those ancestors, when hollow tears ripped
their faces.

Come, come, dance with those ancestors, when only the extended
family operated.

Come, come, dance with those ancestors, when creativity spouted
out...

Wade in the Water, Look Over Jordan, Go Down Mosses.

Come, come, dance with those ancestors, when self-refueling and
self-generating stood abreast while the race root bonded.

Come, come, dance with those ancestors, when the two played chess,
the pawn won the game.

-29-

Part III

Part III views the growth of a child experiencing oneself in search of answers on various levels.

H is in search for his humanity in trying to cement his own place within his environment as it relates to society.

Part III

Anchored On Solid Shores
The Knock
Civilization
Time
The Teacher
Growth
Gone
Destiny With Death
Enchantment through Wisdom
Image
He's Gone

The Knock

Today, a knock left an emptiness in my heart.

A mind without a thought.

A knock that brought reality from fantasy land.

An empty road to freedom without sparkling light.

A knock that brought a smile without the welcome.

The door opened, the knocker entered into the castle, summoning this unwanted body into court.

There was a stillness that generated through the air at the messenger placed a dressed white, engraved envelope, folded in triple copies, into my hands.

He paced down the street, leaving my body pressing against the door.

-32-

Civilization

A racial child cannot fathom the pain within America, until one day he looks beyond where the slant lies.

The child perceives only the encompassing organized structure that rules the society internalized with his ancestors' values.

The child's confused identify unfolds as the masked slope is viewed on a plain.

The child reaches for a sense of being as he is searching for his humanity.

He tries to restore what his ancestors have destroyed.

He steps into reality to find he has befriended the beast.

He tries to sensitize his surrounding with nature.

Dehumanization, stolen values, and those his ancestors have slain are pushed into his subconsciousness.

Time

Another year has surely gone, leaving memories untouched by the passing of time.

The cold icy snow will soon give rise to spring.

The explosion of life will surround us once more.

As it slowly drifts into the warmest period of the year, many will retreat to their summer houses.

With the blinking of an eye, the leaves will descend upon us once again.

The time of hibernation will swiftly creep within our midst.

And another year will have gone without my consciousness.

The Teacher

There are no pranks in thank you, just an appreciation.

There is no shame to frame kindness, just an observation.

There will be a perception of caring and sharing when sensitivity rings true.

There will be wiping or drying tears, unless feelings hold the heart.

An ear to hear can perceive the tear not yet dripping.

There is no strength unless humbleness rings near.

A tender hand holds endless strength.

To hear the hunger and share your pear is the thought.

There will be no education until the receiver perceives.

There will be no teaching until the implementation goal has been received.

There are no cool rules without the foundation tool.

There is no joy when toy traps cripple the admiration road.

There should be no glorious gratification when the gift of thank you have been omitted.

There should be no jubilation when humiliation has touched a soul.

There should be no criticism without a constructive preventive.

There should be no harsh tone when a soft voice can rise to the occasion.

Growth

Growth comes sometimes with moving.
Friends left behind sometimes feel a deep void.
Growth takes its place.
A child grows to manhood and the mother cries.
A lover outgrows a compassion, and the other cries.
Somewhere in between, growth has taken its own direction.

Gone

One day you turn to touch the body that occupies the space near you.

As a bird that flies with the wind, it will no longer be touchable.

The time would have come for it to depart.

Wondering why in a melancholy state will only sadden you deeper.
If there is to be an impact of memories with this relationship, guard
and treasure the happiness that we have shared together.

I chose you when our paths met because the time of choosing was
upon me.

Lifestyle double curiosity was laid to rest shortly before venturing into
the unknown.

The affectionate state of your facial expression that fostered this initial
interest has been enhanced by the wittiness of your mind.

Yes, the goal has been accomplished, the challenge met, rewards
gratification yields not.

Yielding not stress, only intriguing adventure upon this journey.
The shoes are laced to walk when it becomes unbearable with only
memories of happiness remaining.

Destiny With Death

When there are limitations on time, each moment becomes an epoch,
an epoch that cries for another moment to finish the undone tasks.
Each stage is set for that particular moment, because there is no
tomorrow.

Only yesterday and what can be implanted in that given moment.
A stage that is set for a moment of sadness, with an epithet of
heroism.

A farewell wish guidance to inflame the minds of innocence.

It is a time of pensiveness with loved ones.

When dreams have portrayed the impossible, there is a moment of
solidarity with the mind reflecting upon the past.

Enchantment through Wisdom

Eighty-five shines through five.
Children throw kisses without misses.
Her hands held wrinkles in wisdom strength.
Children's hands flashed in the air, while eyes dashed in amazement.

Eighty-five shines through five.
Starlight sparkles to sight.
Little eyes saucer-wide, "Oh my little angels," softly spoken.
Twilight zone trance, age five, alive. "Mother Winslow."

Eighty-five shines through five.
Generation gaps enriched this legacy.
True to form, this grand moment will spill itself into their history.
Love eyes, Martin's eyes, hands cotton soft.

Eighty-five shines through five.
Measure this moment, children treasure to be retold.
Mother Winslow breathing on tomorrow's legacy.
Children's saucer eyes respecting the elder generation.

Image

Your image crossed…
I wanted to touch you.
I stopped and purchased a few memories.
Your very special corner echoed red roses in a vase.
This image traced away the unpleasantness upon your tombstone.

He's Gone

He was here, now he's gone.
He touched my soul, now he's gone.
He shared his thoughts, now he's gone.
He shared his pains, now he's gone.
He shared his dreams, now he's gone.
He shared his wishes, now he's gone.
He shared his promises, now he's gone.
He was here, now he's gone.

The Coming of Dawn

For every rainbow, there is a cloud.
For every cloud, there is a brighter day.
For each pain, there is a joy to rise.
For every death, there is life born.
For every weakness, there is strength unseen.
For every lie, there is a truth seeker.

IV

Part IV of the text revisits the future of a society through innocence, molding us into "Faith."

Their-determination is implemented through established purpose.

Their needs are met through cooperative economics.

Children are swaying and playing, prancing and a dancing, forever friends.

They are jumping two by two, swaying the rope of hope…

Each poem tells its own story, whether one of inner self-environmental

Observation, harsh reality experiences, or the survival of a people's need to pull together. There is a story waiting to be heard in each of us, except that life sometimes is held together through one line of poetry.

While the author articulates a bit of one one's life, it is a book with elements of cultural diversity and social changes that impact individual development. It informs and inspires with a bit of underlying courage to the reader who may have a similar path as it does with a possibility renewal in "Resolutions," one's future filled with great expectations,

Part IV

High Values on the Process of Living

The Legacy

Strong filled with fire.
Sharing was his mission.
Future generations will exemplify his dreams.
They will put his dream's load on the road and mission on them.
Strong filled with fire.
Sharing was his mission.
He tended his soil and until no more.
He loved the land where he cropped to share,

Strong filled with fire.
Sharing was his mission.
He loved his dogs as he raised his hogs.
He shared his hogs with the needy, but he kept his dear dogs nearby.

Strong was his fired.
Sharing was his mission.
With four generations anchored at his footsteps he departed.
At that moment, the earth stood still.

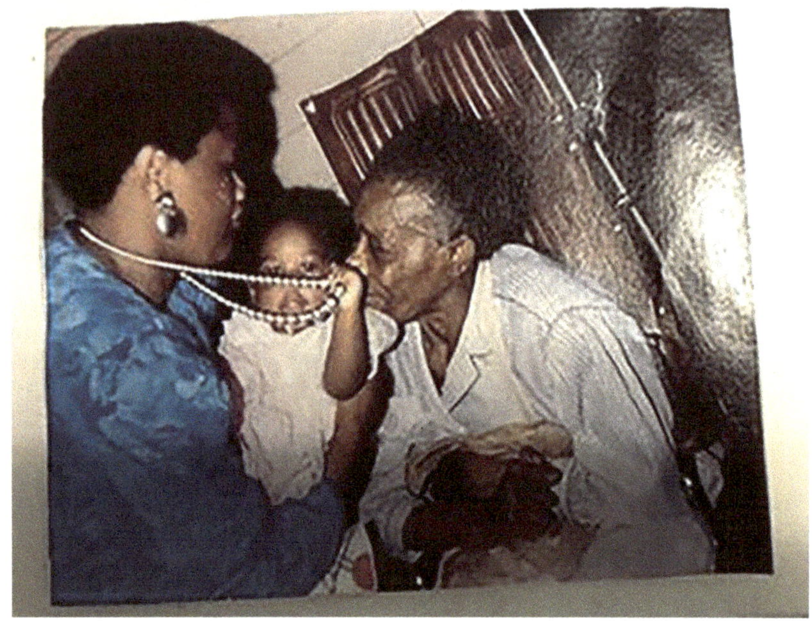

The Timing

We laughed, we cried, we embraced, because it was the time.

We held hands when the sun brought light through the dawn because it was the time.

When the trees shadowed the earth with midnight, the moon gave us fullness, because it was the time.

With love, you danced my steps as our hears blended; yes, it was the time.

With love, you danced my steps as our hearts blended; yes, it was the time.

When the stars sparked our souls, we celebrated with gladness; the emptiness was no more, it was the time.

Now let not journey be in solitude; rejoice with me, it is the time.

Kwanzaa

Kwanzaa is a self-determination act, a self-conscious statement connecting African-American people culturally.

Kwanzaa seeks to rebuild the family, the community, the nation, by enriching the culture through an African values connection.

Kwanzaa was created by Ron Karenga.

The Black Liberation Movement believed that African-Americans should return to their ancestors' roots.

Kwanzaa seeks to connect African-Americans to the motherland. Kwanzaa calls for a united front for those who wish to enhance the African-American life style.

African-Americans must struggle to control their destiny by employing seven principles of Kwanzaa.

Kwanzaa helps to demonstrate and reconfirm our African heritage.

Kwanzaa is not a religious holiday, it is cultural.

Kwanzaa reinforces the bond between African-Americans.

Harvest

People gathered in rope sacks, gathering in the crop.
The first fruit day celebration is coming.
Prize fruits will anchor the table.
People will eat and drink merrily.

People gathered in rope sacks, gathering in the crop.
People cease to argue.
Enemies and friends drink from the same cup.
Spiritual healing captivating the mood.

People gathered in rope sacks, gathering in the crop.
People transcend the highest ideas and values in mankind.
People giving thanks for the closing of the year, another beginning.
People seeking a harmonious relationship with God, the Creator.

People gathered in rope sacks, gathered in the crop.
People are bonding with collective work and responsibility.
People are renewing, strengthening, rejoicing, and reaffirming their relationship.
People embracing only harmonious thoughts with his harvest time.

The Connection

Africans worship the Creator, not ancestors.

Respect the age and character of those ancestors.

Revere the ancestors who created worthy role models.

Ancestors are generation's linkage.

Africans worship the Creator, the ancestors.

Honor the ancestor's deed and how the community was blessed with their presence.

Ancestors receive immortality by the Creator based upon character on earth.

Ancestors opened and modeled the wombs for the future.

Africans worship the Creator, not ancestors.

Ancestors have paved the past for the future unborn.

Ancestors hold the root that links the new to its heritage.

The new should honor and preserve the linkage that bonds.

Africans worship the Creator, not ancestors.

The new should mirror the pathway.

To ignore is to dishonor the deed, depriving the unborn of a rich and irreplaceable legacy.

To acknowledge is to praise a legacy that will guide the new through libation.

Umoja

Umoja—the gentleness of togetherness, holding unbreakable circle.
Umoja—unifies the family, enriching the culture through the family's legacy.

Umoja—the creation of oneness through sameness, an intertwining circle and unbreakable bond.

Umoja—an ethical shopping code stamped within the kingdom.
Umoja—the ultimate demonstration of brotherhood and sisterhood.

Umoja, Umoja… (Unity, #1)

The race wholeness moves with unity.

The whole stands in harmony, connected and joined as one.

The unity moves as a brick, a solid brick.

One that will not be wreck.

-53-

Kujichagulia

Kujichagulia—gathering to define one's self, to amplify one being.

Kujichagulia—gathering to harpoon one's forces.

Kujichagulia—gathering and expounding on the ancient roots. Kujichagulia—echoing the civilization that created the five Cradles. Kujichagulia—gathering to authenticate one culture.

Kujichagulia—shaping and gathering one's image.

Kujichagulia—gathering to reconstruct after the holocaust of enslave-ment.

Kujichagulia—gathering to engrave the ancient pyramid of thoughts. Kujichagulia—gathering to discuss the basis created knowledge of time's oneness.

Kujichagulia—gathering and speaking from the table of oneness. Kujichagulia—gathering with fullness to say "I Am." Kujichagulia —re-establishing the depth of time.

Kujichagulia—gathering to speak one's own truth.

Kujichagulia—gathering, stepping in fours, singing the message of the ancestors.

Kujichagulia—gathering to embrace one's goodness.

Kujichagulia, Kujichagulia… (Co-operative Responsibility, #2) Dancing, upward through you.

Through you, I will not fall.

I stand because you hold me.

If you leave, bit and pieces of me leaves with you.

Let me not be destroyed.

Kujichagulia

Ujima

Ujima—coming together on common interest.

Ujima—sharing our future collectively because we must determine and enrich our destiny.

Ujima—working collectively to build the community by sharing responsibility to maintain the highest form of ethics.

Ujima—enriching the community by solving each other's problem.
Ujima—accepting responsibility through cooperative behavior bene- fiting the whole.

Ujima—seeking to enhance the future by being responsible collectively.

Ujima—teaching youth how to be cooperative and share each other's failures and successes.

Ujima—helps establish our fundamental future that will endure forever.

Ujima—seeks to restore collectively the destruction that occurred through the holocaust of slavery.

Ujima—moves collectively, responding to the needs within the community.

Ujima—responds to others as self.

Ujima—allows one to plow the depth of his being as related to the community, combing as the unique one.

Ujima, Ujima

Fire In My Bones

(Collective Responsibility, #3)

Bring forth me with those who will connect me.
The strength of me is connected through the whole.

Ujamaa

Ujamaa—this is the prime time of wealth.
Ujamaa—people sharing work through solid commitment.
Ujamaa—community obtaining wealth through shared responsibility.
Ujamaa—expressing human equality, domination does not rule in
this wide community.
Ujamaa—emphasizing mankind's well-being; happiness shared
through interaction of social wealth.
Ujamaa—priority has been given to human dignity.
Ujamaa—nothing meek as it seeks resources through the community.
Ujamaa—emphasizes self-reliance.
Ujamaa—working cooperatively without exploitation.
Ujamaa—provides meaningful and decent ways to man's dignity.
Ujamaa—shopping the color code.
Ujamaa—seeding and succeeding in your own community.
Ujamaa—the implementation of self-consciousness awareness
when each person responds to the community's needs.
Ujamaa, Ujamaa

(Cooperative Economics #4)

The ship of one is built through others.
When one succeeds, others have touched the anchor.
Communities are built on reinforcement.

Black Wall Street and Rosewood come from forced isolation upon a people.

We can and will rise again.

Nia, Nia

Me, my being, Nia, Nia.

Here I am, Nia, Nia.

Winning, spinning, glorifying, Nia.

Correct me, connect me to the whole.

Coming, going, expressing the greatness of a people.

Promoting, preserving, expanding, and guarding the legacy of a
people.

Recognizing, respecting the humanity that flows with significant
historical contribution.

Nia, Nia, freedom connecting chain links to the whole.

I am whole through you, connect me.

We are one, Nia, Nia.

(Purpose, #5)

The community purpose is established through you and I.

We are connected through the community's purpose.

The purpose of the community is to forward a plan for all.

Kuumba

Kuumba—sparkling beauty, the glistening that sings.

Kuumba—captivating mankind as related to the cosmic earth.

Kuumba—restoring the reins, revitalizing the earthly self.

Kuumba—producing touchless thoughts to shine with gleam.

Kuumba—one being yields to magnify beauty.

Kuumba—serving the future by being harmonious with nature.

Kuumba—building for eternity.

Kuumba—players redesigning layers of destruction for reconstruction.

Kuumba—an external ton of beauty, conceived and constructed through Ron.

Kuumba—gleaming, sparkling, shining from the birth cradle.

Kuumba, Kuumba…

(Creativity, #6)

It is the art which dances in my head.

It pushes me forward, demanding me to dig deeper.

To create things never conceived.

It is a world of beauty dances to jump out of me.

Imani

There is an answer yet unconceived, Imani, Imani the Creator watches over his kingdom.

The elders wait patiently with wisdom.

The protective shield patches the torn whole.

Let not pretend, be innovative and invent.

There is an answer yet unconceived, Imani, Imani, the Creator watches over his kingdom.

Struggling to free ourselves politically, the new will not outlast the past, imitation outdated.

The gentleness of our Creator will guide us with smoothness.

Our unique contributions will fill the history story with its own special truth.

There is an answer yet unconceived, Imani, Imani, values with significant benefits.

Faith in the Creator, strength faith on one's self.

The impossible becomes possible; without it the struggle ceases.

The growth of the race depends upon faith's depth.

There is an answer yet unconceived, Imani, Imani, with spiritually centering around the Creator.

The Creator allows us to become victorious within our struggles.

Fire In My Bones

Maximum thoughts' positiveness allows us to pursue the depth of faith.

Let us sing as we step out on faith with the Creator.

Imani, Imani…

(Faith, #7)

Faith

Picture children 's future, setting the pathway for the spring.
Creating changes for the cominvg generation.
Their own generation establishing the future purpose.
Children jumping two by two, swinging the rope of hope.

Inspiration's smiles line with tomorrow, a row of hope.
Children are faith creators.
Parents transform doubt elements within any child.
Children jumping two by two, swinging the rope of hope.

Their self-determination implemented through established purpose.
Their needs are met through cooperative economics.
Children are swaying and playing, prancing and a' dancing forever friends.
They are jumping two by two, swinging the rope of hope.

Unity binds their mind as one, forever.
Brainy heads creating needed change.
Their eyes are trickled stars dancing and a' prancing anew.
They are still jumping two by two, swinging the rope of hope.

Strength through Harambee

Harambee—power force within unity strength.

Standing tall, embraced with many, you shall not fall.

An intertwining circle, reinforced with inner strength.

Sisters searching, reaching, and touching the harmony of oneness.

Harambee—a power force within unity strength.

Runners with strength, honoring their ancestors in multiple of seven.

Trudging on, struggling together in unity.

Ancestors' wisdom guiding and moving us into the future.

Harambee—a power force within unity strength.

Submitting willingly to the Creator, demonstrating the Nguzo Sasa Principle.

Sisters serving as models within the content of their lives.

Sisters reassessing and recommitting their lives to the family, the community, and the nation.

Harambee—a power force within unity strength.

Remembering the ancestors, rejoicing with oneness, struggling on, trudging the richness of tomorrow.

Power sisters greeting with unity, gathering untamed thoughts, building a new world free of game.

Harambee—a power force within unity strength.

An Ancient Path

Ancient African woman, let the middle passage tell the story.
Race's scare bellows the quivering stomach.
Hurt eyes gleam, dew morning.
River blue flows red.

Ancient African woman, let the middle passage tell the story.
Women sway astute pattern rules.
Women's wisdom embedded cried on future.
New land filled with sand of tears.

Ancient African Woman, let the middle passage tell the story.
An anxious child's face, faced not with wisdom.
Triumphal time echoes tomorrow not.
Hollow tree story's eyes flow red.

Ancient African woman, let the middle passage tell the story.
Yesterday's child shame chilled not.
The ecstatic oblivious pain plunked away.
An ancient path flows in river red, anchored on the middle passage.

The Ultimate

Man and woman relate as two individuals coming into one.

Forces are pushing, pulling, trying to submerge.

Each moment is an utopia of infinite happiness.

As the water from the mountain connects with the mouth of the river; the present has been submerged into the future.

A generation springing remorse or a lamb of happiness.

Son

In the spirit of Harambee, separation has come.

Ancestors behold the pathway.

Let not the family, the community, and the nation eye with tears.

The Creator has summoned this departure.

In the spirit of Harambee, God brought you forth.

You sprang forth in deep delt Georgia on a bright autumn morning
etched in love!

We merged on the northern shore from the coast of Florida.

Amidst your siblings, you grew into a giant.

In the spirit of Harambee, your family shall see you again.

When you appeared, your sister's whole being ruffled in smiles.

Your family, your brothers, embraced you with love.

God, the Creator, loved you first and best and now has called you
into his kingdom.

In the spirit of Harambee, rest in peace.

God, the Creator, has carried you home.

In time, we shall see each other again.

Until then, Harambee, Harambee, the family.

Life

Thirty-two years we shared.
One future clone, name dangles he.
Smooth, immaculate dresser, rest he.
Diamonds, gold, proudly he wore.

Thirty-two years we shared.
One Native African bridges the middle passage.
The incredible capture without bandage.
Friends first, wedding bells on river shells.

Thirty-two years we shared.
When the end came, you held my hands, tides overrode.
God blessed us with new life, he tarried far and near.
God has shown his blessings, so we were not stressed.

Thirty-two years we shared.
When the end came, your shoulders were ever in sight.
Comforting words echoed from your lips.
Your presence lifted the sadness from my heart.

Resolutions

Ringing out the old and bringing in the new with unmet last year's resolutions.

Determine to set forth new path, a time to enact decisions through resolutions by expressing the hopes, the wishes, one feels so deeply. Yet a time to wonder whether to expire with resolutions and transform time to each given moment.

The atmosphere is high with hope, dreams are plentiful, and reality lies somewhere in between the garish lights on this newborn day.

The sharp, shrilling whistling sound sweeps the room at the stroke of midnight, welcoming in the New Year.

Couple are uttering resolutions with great expectations, assuring each other of promises to be met this year that shall be only kept for this day.

One has gone, another one well soon disappear and when the next arises, this self shall be known a little better.

Fire in My Bones

In a world of parting and pain, Ollie Marshall-Rico gives voices to her agony through Fire in My Bones with her poetic verses. She writes through life's observations and personal experiences with a demanding cry to cope with different challenges that are sometimes forced upon us beyond our control.

Touching on the concept that racial unity is strength and exhorting us to learn from our part as we respect our ancestors, elders, and history, she explores and reaffirms her heritage ad she shares her deep and abiding faith in our Creator, God. ''Revere the ancestor,'' she says, "and honor God."

In creating her poetic expression, she releases her hate, injustice, and racial imbalance of discrimination she has experienced all her life, despite the many contributions to the betterment of our society.

Fire in My Bones is a cry to be heard, a cry to be appreciated, a cry for release of the pain of the unfairness inflicted upon Ollie Marshall-Rico's very soul.

-75-